What's in this book

This book belongs to

_____

奥运会 The Olympic Games

学习内容 Contents

沟通 Communication

说说体育运动
Talk about sports

背景介绍：
奥林匹克运动会，简称奥运会，是国际上影响力最大的综合性运动会。奥运会分为夏季奥林匹克运动会、冬季奥林匹克运动会、残疾人奥林匹克运动会、青年奥林匹克运动会等等。本书主要介绍夏季奥林匹克运动会。

生词 New words

最	most
开始	to start
第	(marker of ordinal numerals)
号	date
跑	to run
走	to walk
快	fast
体育	sport
篮球	basketball
羽毛球	badminton
跳	to jump
慢	slow

雅典奥林匹克室内自行车赛场，2004年雅典夏季奥运会室内自行车比赛场馆

伦敦奥林匹克体育场，2012年伦敦夏季奥运会开、闭幕式及田径比赛场馆

里约奥林匹克网球中心，2016年里约夏季奥运会网球比赛场馆

希腊举办了最早的奥林匹克运动会。

The very first Olympic Games were held in Greece.

搜集一位奥运会奖牌得主的资料
并介绍他/她

Research an Olympic medal winner
and talk about him/her

北京奥运会
Beijing Olympic Games

参考答案：
1 They are the Athens Olympic Velodrome, the London Stadium and the Olympic Tennis Centre in Rio./They are all sports venues for the Olympic Games.
2 The Olympic sports events were held there.
3 Yes, I like watching football./No, I do not like watching sports.

Get ready

1 Do you know what these buildings are?

2 Do you know what events were held in these buildings?

3 Do you like watching sports events?

776 BC

zuì zǎo de
最早的

表示没有同类的人或事物能够超过时，可以用"最"来形容，如"最好的"和"最快的"。

故事大意：
浩浩和同学们正在参观一个介绍奥运会历史的展览，并在参观结束后做了报告。

左边两幅图和右下角的图展示的是奥林匹亚——古代奥运会的遗址。右上角的图展示的是古希腊人比赛跑步的场景。

参考问题和答案：
1 What do you think the place in the photos is? (It was where the ancient Olympic Games were held.)
2 When were the first ever Olympic Games held? (In 776 BC.)

两三千年前，希腊举办了最早的奥林匹克运动会（奥运会）。

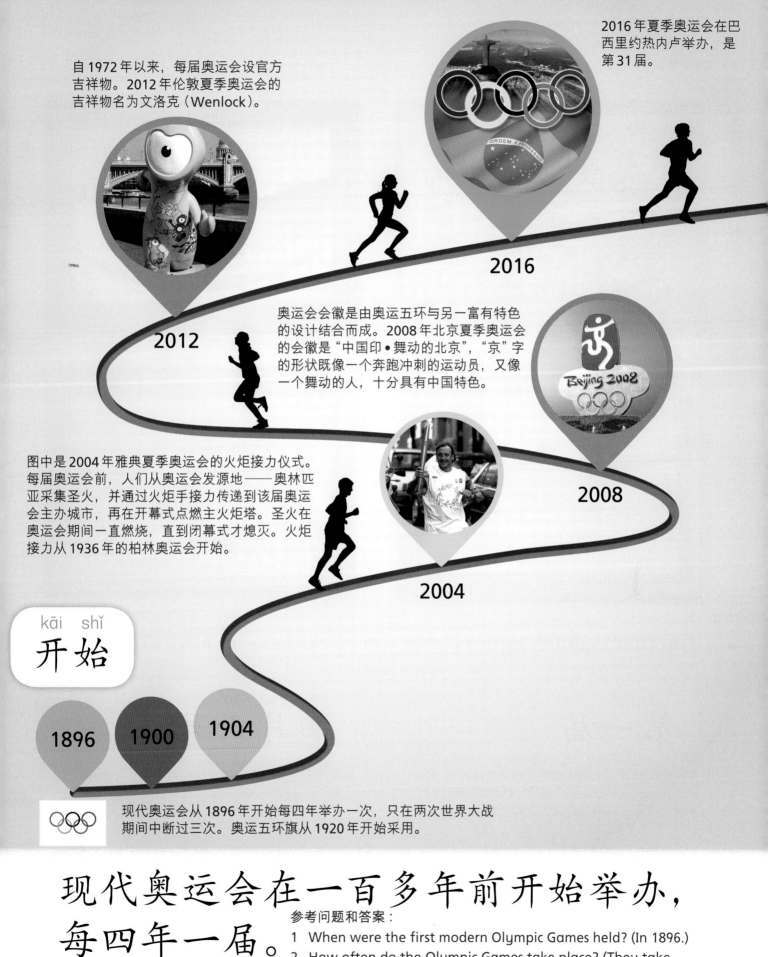

2016年夏季奥运会在巴西里约热内卢举办，是第31届。

自1972年以来，每届奥运会设官方吉祥物。2012年伦敦夏季奥运会的吉祥物名为文洛克（Wenlock）。

2016

2012

奥运会会徽是由奥运五环与另一富有特色的设计结合而成。2008年北京夏季奥运会的会徽是"中国印·舞动的北京"，"京"字的形状既像一个奔跑冲刺的运动员，又像一个舞动的人，十分具有中国特色。

2008

图中是2004年雅典夏季奥运会的火炬接力仪式。每届奥运会前，人们从奥运会发源地——奥林匹亚采集圣火，并通过火炬手接力传递到该届奥运会主办城市，再在开幕式点燃主火炬塔。圣火在奥运会期间一直燃烧，直到闭幕式才熄灭。火炬接力从1936年的柏林奥运会开始。

2004

kāi shǐ
开始

1896 **1900** **1904**

现代奥运会从1896年开始每四年举办一次，只在两次世界大战期间中断过三次。奥运五环旗从1920年开始采用。

现代奥运会在一百多年前开始举办，每四年一届。

参考问题和答案：

1 When were the first modern Olympic Games held? (In 1896.)
2 How often do the Olympic Games take place? (They take place every four years.)
3 Where were the 2008 Olympic Games held? (In Beijing.)

The **first** ever Olympic Games were held here on **6 April** 1896.

dì yī jiè
第一届

第一届现代奥运会在雅典的泛雅典娜体育场（the Panathenaic Stadium）举行。该体育场在古代用来举办纪念女神雅典娜的泛雅典娜运动会。

sì yuè liù hào
四月六号

指某一天的具体日期时，可以用"号"或者"日"，如"六号"或"六日"。

第一届在一八九六年四月六号举行，也是在希腊。

参考问题和答案：
1 In which year were the first modern Olympic Games held? (1896.)
2 On which date were the first modern Olympic Games held? (6 April.)
3 The first modern Olympic Games were held in the Panathenaic Stadium. Do you know where it is? (It is in Athens, Greece.)

奥运五环象征着五大洲的团结和世界
各地运动员共聚一堂。

| 射箭 | 田径 | 羽毛球 | 篮球 | 沙滩排球 | 拳击 | 独木舟（激流障碍赛） |

| 独木舟（静水竞速赛） | 小轮车 | 越野自行车 | 公路自行车 | 场地自行车 |

| 跳水 | 马术盛装舞步赛 | 马术三项赛 | 马术障碍赛 | 击剑 | 足球 | 高尔夫球 | 竞技体操 |

| 韵律体操 | 蹦床 | 手球 | 曲棍球 | 柔道 | 现代五项 |

| 赛艇 | 橄榄球 | 帆船 | 射击 | 游泳 | 花样游泳 |

| 乒乓球 | 跆拳道 | 网球 | 铁人三项 | 室内排球 | 水球 | 举重 | 自由式摔跤 | 古典式摔跤 |

今天，奥运会的体育项目有四十
多个。

参考问题和答案：

1 How many sports events can you see in the picture? (There are 41 events.)
2 Can you name any of them? (There are archery, athletics, badminton,
basketball ...)

lán qiú
篮球

yǔ máo qiú
羽毛球

zǒu
走

pǎo
跑

tiào
跳

参考问题和答案:
Can you name all the sports events here?
(Yes, they are basketball, badminton, pole
vaulting, sprinting and race walking.)

篮球、羽毛球、跳高、跑步、竞
走……你都可以在奥运会上看到。

màn
慢

"快"和"慢"是一对反义词。

kuài
快

不管是男还是女，是快还是慢，大家都是好朋友。

参考问题和答案：

What do you think is the most important thing about the Olympic Games besides winning a medal? (It is to do one's best in the competition./It is to compete fairly and make friends with people from different places.)

Let's think

1 Which one of these is the symbol of the Olympic Games? Circle the correct letter.

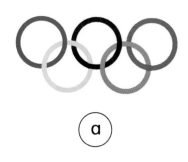

(a)

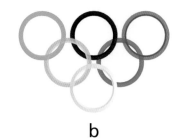

b

c

2 Write the years of the Olympic Games.   可结合第5页内容，让学生说说列出的每一届奥运会都在哪里举办。

2004	2008	2012	2016	2020
希腊雅典	中国北京	英国伦敦	巴西里约热内卢	日本东京

3 What are the children doing? Tick the Olympic sports.   提醒学生参考第7页的奥运比赛项目。

 ✔

 ✔

 ✔

 ✔

New words

1 Learn the new words.

延伸活动：
让学生看图，指着图中人物说话。如：这个男孩最快，艾文第二，
这个男孩第三，伊森最慢。浩浩打篮球。玲玲打羽毛球。

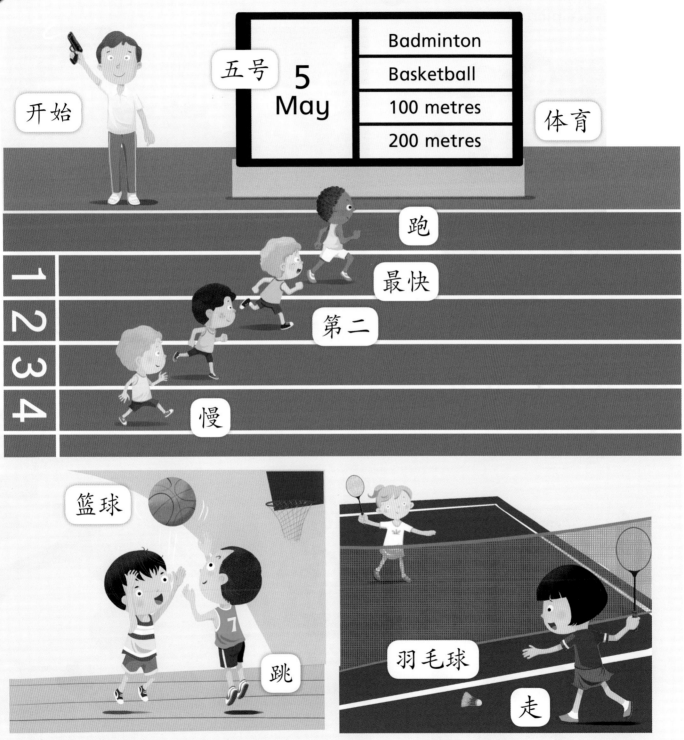

五号	5 May	Badminton
		Basketball
		100 metres
		200 metres

开始 · 体育 · 跑 · 最快 · 第二 · 慢 · 篮球 · 跳 · 羽毛球 · 走

2 Listen to your teacher and act out the words.

听听说说 Listen and say

1 Listen and tick the correct pictures.

1

✓

2

✓

3

✓

2 Look at the pictures. Listen to the story ar

Olympic Games

一、二、三，开始！

谁最快？

长颈鹿，你个子高，你打篮球。

猴子，你喜欢跳，你打羽毛球。

第二题参考问题和答案：

1 Who is the winner of the running competition? (The horse.)
2 Which sports event would you like to take part in in your school sports meeting? (I'd like to take part in the long jump/running competition.)

J.

你看，马最快，跑第一。老虎跑第二。

老虎怎么比马慢？

狮子爷爷，您慢慢走。

我最慢，你们都比我快。

3 Write the letters. Role-play with your friend.

a 走　b 跑　c 跳　d 篮球

1

笑啊、__c__ 啊，我真快乐。

来，我们一起打 __d__。

2

跑、跑、__b__，我第一，你第二。

3

4

我们 __a__ 回家。

Task

What sports do you and your friends like? Do a survey and write your names.

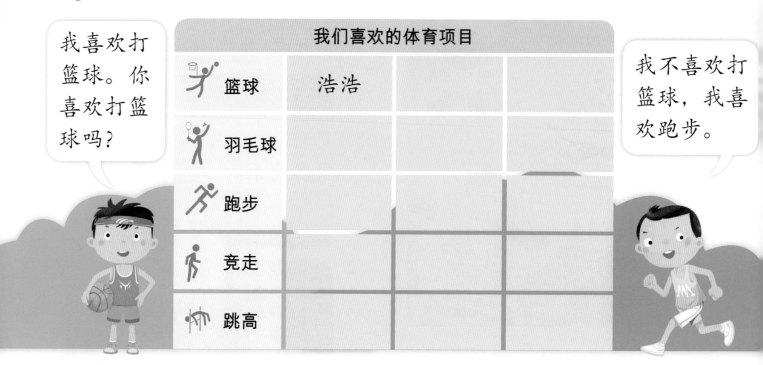

我喜欢打篮球。你喜欢打篮球吗？

我不喜欢打篮球，我喜欢跑步。

我们喜欢的体育项目			
篮球	浩浩		
羽毛球			
跑步			
竞走			
跳高			

Game

Listen to your teacher. Repeat the words in white. For the ones in black, repeat and act them out.

Chant

Listen and say.

延伸活动：
将儿歌歌词与 Old MacDonald
had a farm 的曲调结合起来唱诵。

多做运动身体好，

真呀真开心！

我们一起来赛跑，

看谁第一名。

你跑得快，我跑得慢，

第一第二第三名。

大家一起来赛跑，

真呀真开心！

生活用语 Daily expressions

加油！
Come on!

好球！
Good shot!

写一写 Write

1 Trace and write the characters.

走

提醒学生，“走”字的“竖”是分开两笔写的。

走 走 走 走

跑

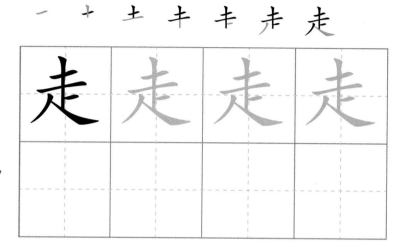

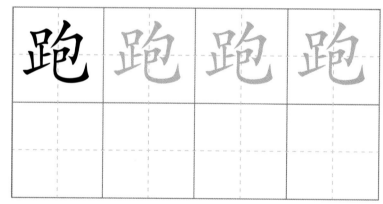

跑 跑 跑 跑

2 Write and say. 提醒学生，两题的第一个空都与年龄有关，第二个空都与动作有关。

他一__岁__。
他喜欢__走__。

她三__岁__。
她喜欢__跑__。

3 Read and circle the wrong words, then write the correct ones. There is one mistake in each line.

提醒学生先将段落完整读一遍，然后观察图片，再将每行文字仔细对照图片，圈出错误的字并改正。完成后，再通读改正的段落，看看是否与图片内容完全对应。

星期六(晚)上，伊森、艾文和	1	早
浩浩一起在公园玩。艾文(走)在最	2	跑
前面。浩浩第(一)，在艾文后面。	3	二
伊森(走)在最后面，他是第三。	4	跑
艾文很高兴，因为(她)最快。	5	他

拼音输入法 Pinyin input

Circle the wrong characters in the messages and choose the correct ones. Write the letters.

a 画画 b 笔 c 马

In Pinyin input, tones are usually not required. Therefore, one Pinyin syllable can generate a list of characters with different tones. Because of this, it is important to remember the form of the desired character.

1

你有什么文具？

我有(鼻)和尺子。

b

2

你喜欢什么动物？

我喜欢(妈)。

c

3

你星期二打篮球吗？

不，我星期二(花花)。

a

多元学习 Connections

2008年北京夏季奥运会是第29届奥运会，口号是"同一个世界，同一个梦想"，吉祥物是福娃。五位福娃配合奥运五环，名字取"北京欢迎你"的谐音，分别命名为"贝贝"（鲤鱼）、"晶晶"（熊猫）、"欢欢"（奥林匹克圣火）、"迎迎"（藏羚羊）和"妮妮"（燕子）。另外，福娃的每一个形象分别表示与天、地、水、火和森林的联系。

1 The 2008 Olympic Games were held in Beijing. Learn about the Games.

Beijing 2008

From 8 to 24 August, 10,942 athletes from 204 countries and areas competed in 302 events.

The main venues

the Beijing National Stadium
(the Bird's Nest)

the Beijing National Aquatics Centre
(the Water Cube)

2 Do you know the five mascots? Their names form the sentence 'bei jing huan ying ni', which means 'welcome to Beijing'. Match them to the animals/element they represent.

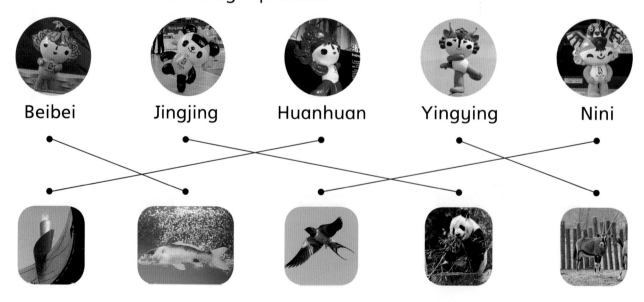

Beibei   Jingjing   Huanhuan   Yingying   Nini

Yelena Isinbayeva 是俄罗斯的撑杆跳运动员，她是 2004 和 2008 年的奥运会冠军。Lin Dan 是中国的羽毛球运动员，他是 2008 和 2012 年的奥运会男子单打冠军。Roger Federer 是瑞士的网球运动员，他是 2008 年的奥运会硬地双打冠军。Usain Bolt 是牙买加的跑步运动员，他曾在 2008、2012 和 2016 年的奥运会上拿过多项男子短跑冠军，并在 2016 年的奥运会上获得一项男子 4×100 米接力冠军。

1 When did these athletes win their gold medals in the Olympic Games? Do an online research. Then match them to their names. Write the letters.

| a Lin Dan | b Roger Federer | c Usain Bolt | d Yelena Isinbayeva |

2 Research an Olympic medal winner that you like. Paste his/her photo and tell your friend about him/her.

Paste the photo here.

我最喜欢……
他/她很高/矮/胖/瘦。
他/她的脸圆圆的/方方的。
他/她会跑步/打球/跳高/……
……年，他/她是第一/二/三。

温习 Checkpoint

学生可以一边模仿图中的动作，一边完成图中的任务。

1 Say the words and the sentences and write the characters. Then draw your face on one of the pictures on the right.

第一天

一、二、三，开始！

我喜欢跑。

100m

我喜欢跳。

这是什么球？

你会跳高吗？

400m

今天是第一天，七月八号。

我跑步第一！我真快乐。

第二天

一、二、三，开始！

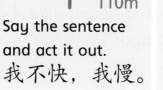

110m

Say 'sport' in Chinese. 体育

这是我的。我跳高第一！

Say the sentence and act it out. 我不快，我慢。

Say 'the ninth' in Chinese. 第九

Write the character.

走

Write the character.

1500m

跑

评核方法：

学生两人一组，互相考察评价表内单词和句子的听说读写。交际沟通部分由老师朗读要求，学生再互相对话。如果达到了某项技能要求，则用色笔将星星或小辣椒涂色。

2 Work with your friend. Colour the stars and the chillies.

Words	说	读	写
最	☆	☆	🌶
开始	☆	☆	🌶
第	☆	☆	🌶
号	☆	☆	🌶
跑	☆	☆	☆
走	☆	☆	☆
快	☆	☆	☆
体育	☆	🌶	🌶
篮球	☆	🌶	🌶

Words and sentences	说	读	写
羽毛球	☆	🌶	🌶
跳	☆	🌶	🌶
慢	☆	🌶	🌶
希腊举办了最早的奥林匹克运动会。	☆	🌶	🌶

Talk about sports	☆

3 What does your teacher say?

评核建议：

根据学生课堂表现，分别给予"太棒了！(Excellent!)"、"不错！(Good!)"或"继续努力！(Work harder!)"的评价，再让学生圈出左侧对应的表情，以记录自己的学习情况。

My teacher says ...

分享 Sharing

延伸活动：
1 学生用手遮盖英文，读中文单词，并思考单词意思；
2 学生用手遮盖中文单词，看着英文说出对应的中文单词；
3 学生两人一组，尽量运用中文单词复述第4至9页内容。

Words I remember

最	zuì	most
开始	kāi shǐ	to start
第	dì	(marker of ordinal numbers
号	hào	date
跑	pǎo	to run
走	zǒu	to walk
快	kuài	fast
体育	tǐ yù	sport
篮球	lán qiú	basketball
羽毛球	yǔ máo qiú	badminton
跳	tiào	to jump
慢	màn	slow

Other words

前	qián	before
希腊	xī là	Greece
举办	jǔ bàn	to host, to hold
奥林匹克运动会	ào lín pǐ kè yùn dòng huì	the Olympic Games
现代	xiàn dài	modern
多	duō	more than
每	měi	every
届	jiè	session
举行	jǔ xíng	to hold
项目	xiàng mù	event
跳高	tiào gāo	high jump
跑步	pǎo bù	running
竞走	jìng zǒu	race walk
可以	kě yǐ	to be able to
不管	bù guǎn	regardless of

OXFORD
UNIVERSITY PRESS

Oxford University Press is a department of the University of Oxford.
It furthers the University's objective of excellence in research, scholarship,
and education by publishing worldwide. Oxford is a registered trade mark of
Oxford University Press in the UK and in certain other countries

Published in Hong Kong by
Oxford University Press (China) Limited
39th Floor, One Kowloon, 1 Wang Yuen Street, Kowloon Bay,
Hong Kong

Illustrated by Anne Lee, Ah Lun, KY Chan and Wildman

Photographs for reproduction permitted by Dreamstime.com

China National Publications Import & Export (Group) Corporation is an authorized distributor of
Oxford Elementary Chinese.

Please contact content@cnpiec.com.cn or 86-10-65856782

ISBN: 978-0-19-942996-7

10 9 8 7 6 5 4 3 2

Teacher's Edition
ISBN: 978-0-19-082261-3

10 9 8 7 6 5 4 3 2